WRITINGS TO YOUNG WOMEN FROM

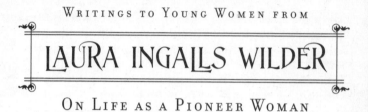

LAURA INGALLS WILDER

ON LIFE AS A PIONEER WOMAN

VOLUME TWO

Laura Ingalls Wilder
Edited by Stephen W. Hines

TOMMY NELSON™
for tweens and teens
A Division of Thomas Nelson Publishers
Since 1798
www.thomasnelson.com

Writings to Young Women from Laura Ingalls Wilder:
On Life as a Pioneer Woman
Volume Two
Adapted from *Little House in the Ozarks*
Copyright © 2006 by Stephen W. Hines

Cover design by Lookout Design, Inc.

Published in Nashville, Tennessee, by Tommy Nelson®, a Division of Thomas Nelson, Inc. Visit us on the Web at www.tommynelson.com.

Tommy Nelson® books may be purchased in bulk for educational, business, fund-raising, or sales promotional use. For information, please e-mail:
SpecialMarkets@ThomasNelson.com.

Scripture quotations are taken from *The Holy Bible, King James Version*.

This book is not in any way sponsored by or affiliated with HarperCollins Publishers, which claims the exclusive right to use the words "Little House" as a trademark. Our use of these words simply and truthfully brings to you the warm personal facts about Laura Ingalls Wilder, America's beloved author, and about her life, times, and beliefs.

Cover photograph credits: Laura's profile (Herbert Hoover Presidential Library), Almanzo, Jell-O® Advertisement (The Kansas State Historical Society), Laura (The Kansas State Historical Society), Maytag® Advertisement (The Kansas State Historical Society), Karo® Advertisement (The Kansas State Historical Society), Laura's kitchen (Herbert Hoover Presidential Library), Laura's window seat (Herbert Hoover Presidential Library), Laura (Herbert Hoover Presidential Library).

Library of Congress Cataloging-in-Publication Data

Wilder, Laura Ingalls, 1867-1957.
   [Prose works. Selections]
   Writings to young women from Laura Ingalls Wilder / Laura Ingalls Wilder ; edited by Stephen W. Hines.
   p. cm.
   ISBN 1-4003-0785-6 (*On Life as A Pioneer Woman*, Volume Two)
   1. Young women—Conduct of life. I. Hines, Stephen W. II. Title.
PS3545.I342A6 2006
814'.52—dc22

2005033723

Printed in the United States of America

06 07 08 09 10 WRZ 9 8 7 6 5 4 3 2 1

CONTENTS

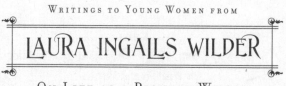

WRITINGS TO YOUNG WOMEN FROM

LAURA INGALLS WILDER

ON LIFE AS A PIONEER WOMAN

VOLUME TWO

FOREWORD

The way people live today has changed so much from the way people lived when the western part of the United States was settled—from approximately 1850 to 1890—that it is hard to present the reality of pioneer life in contrast to life today.

Not only were there no cars and airplanes back then but also there was virtually no such thing as prepackaged food, except for some kinds of hard candy and crackers. Grocery stores, or general stores as they were more commonly called, had great wooden barrels of flour, sugar, molasses, and the like.

Meat came freshly cut or was hunted and killed by the pioneers themselves. To have fried chicken was a special treat that involved killing the chicken, dipping it in scalding hot water, plucking the feathers off, and then holding it over a flame to singe any remaining feathers. The smell of doing this was pungent; you definitely knew your food came from a living animal. Store-bought chicken today often looks as though it was manufactured in a factory, and we don't have to experience the strong smells from preparing it.

Just as preparing food was different, travel was also different and took more time and effort. People traveled very little compared to how much we do now. Ten miles was a long distance for a pioneer. A man driving a wagon might take half a day to go that far; then if he had to come back in the same day, he barely made it home by sundown. By comparison, we can drive ten miles in ten minutes easily!

Horses and donkeys or mules required constant care, shelter, and feed. Caring for such animals was almost a full-time job in itself. Of course, a car requires care, too, but it doesn't eat all the time and smell bad or attract flies.

Yet there were things that made up for the hardships of the old days. When people did finally have time to gather and visit, there were no distractions by way of television, radio, video games, or even record players. People actually talked to one another, and this led to closer relationships and stronger community ties. People relied on one another and were willing to help their neighbors in times of need.

It was not unusual for farmers and their wives to trade work. If a farmer needed to put up a barn, and most of them did, the farmer's friends would "lend a hand," and the barn would be put up in a few days. No money actually changed hands for the work, because they were going to help others put their own barns up, or they might help in harvesting a crop.

Women would have "workings" where they helped each other harvest vegetables from the garden, mostly beans and peas. They would sit and shell peas or "snap" green beans and talk. Very strong friendships formed in this environment where entertainment was limited and the work constant.

Even children did a lot of work. Boys began working with their fathers to learn whatever skills their fathers had, and girls went into training early with their mothers to learn how to be good homemakers. Education was limited for most pioneer children but offered opportunities to get the basics in reading, writing, and arithmetic.

Play was one of the big benefits of going to school back then. At recess, students trooped outside to play games of tag and baseball. Recess took place sometimes three times a day. When the weather was bad, students could entertain themselves by playing tic-tac-toe and checkers inside.

Reading was also an important pastime, and newspapers and magazines were saved and traded between family and friends. Children's books were popular back then, just as they are today. Only there were fewer books, and good books were treasures that were passed down from generation to generation.

Laura Ingalls Wilder lived long enough to see the dawn

of the rocket age, and she was excited about progress and modern inventions, but she never felt these things replaced the traditional moral values of her pioneer days. She said: "Across the years, the old home and its love called to me, and memories of sweet words of counsel came flooding back. . . . Strength to the good will not come from the modern improvements . . . but from the quiet moments and the 'still small voices' of the old home."

External things have changed a lot since pioneer times, but as people we are not that different from the pioneers of Laura's day.

Stephen W. Hines
Editor

ACKNOWLEDGMENTS

First of all, I would like to acknowledge the invaluable aid of my wife, Gwendolyn Joy Hines, in this undertaking. Her persistence in proofreading, titling of articles, and all-around general good advice made this project flow much more smoothly than it would have otherwise.

And my thanks to:
Gordon R. Cuany for obtaining material for me through interlibrary loan.

Jackie Dana for her determined research efforts at the Ellis Library of the University of Missouri at Columbia, Missouri.

Patricia Timberlake, June DeWeese, Margaret Howell, Laurel Boeckman, and Marie Concannon, librarians at the Ellis Library, who answered my questions and allowed me to review highly fragile material.

Suzanne Lippard, library clerk, for her fund of personal

information about Laura Ingalls Wilder and about the people still living who had known her.

Marion Bond, library assistant for the Kansas State Historical Society, for invaluable help in speeding my research.

Dwight Miller, now retired, who as head of the Herbert Hoover Library in West Branch, Iowa, helped me track down archival material.

Bruce Barbour, former publisher of Thomas Nelson Trade Books, for backing the lengthy efforts of *Little House in the Ozarks* from which this current project was adapted.

Bill Watkins, former Senior Editor at Thomas Nelson Trade Books, for his alert eye in going over the manuscript for *Little House in the Ozarks*.

And special thanks to Jennifer Gingerich, Backlist Editor for Tommy Nelson, for making this current project possible.

ONE

FARM LIFE
IN THE OZARKS

*"The land was so poor it would not raise
a stalk of corn over four feet high."*

Let's Visit Mrs. Wilder

FEBRUARY 1918

by John F. Case

Missouri farm folks need little introduction before getting acquainted with Mrs. A. J. Wilder of Rocky Ridge Farm. During the years that she has been connected with this paper—a greater number of years than any other person on the editorial staff—she has taken strong hold upon the esteem and affections of our great family. Mrs. Wilder has lived her life upon a farm. She knows farm folks and their problems as few women who write know them. And having sympathy with the folks whom she serves, she writes well.

The Wilder Home

"Mrs. Wilder is a woman of delightful personality," a neighbor tells me, "and she is a combination of energy and determination. She always is cheery, looking on the bright side. She is her husband's partner in every sense and is fully capable of managing the farm. No woman can make you feel more at home than can Mrs. Wilder, and yet, when the occasion demands, she can be dignity personified. Mrs. Wilder has held high rank in the Eastern Star. Then when a Farm Loan Association was formed at Mansfield, she was made secretary-treasurer. When her report was sent to the Land Bank officials, they told her the papers were perfect and the best sent in." As a final tribute Mrs. Wilder's friend said this: "She gets eggs in the winter when none of her neighbors gets them."

"I was born in a log house within four miles of the legend-haunted Lake Pepin in Wisconsin," Mrs. Wilder wrote when I asked for information about her. "I remember seeing deer that father had killed hanging in the trees about our forest home. When I was four years old, we traveled to the Indian Territory—Fort Scott, Kansas, being our nearest town. [Actually, Laura's memory failed her. The town was Independence, Kansas, much farther to the south.] My childish memories hold the sound of the war whoop, and I see pictures of painted Indians."

Looking at the picture of Mrs. Wilder, which was recently taken, we find it difficult to believe that she is old enough to be the pioneer described. But having confided her age to the editor (not for publication), we must be convinced that it is true. Surely Mrs. Wilder—who is the mother of Rose Wilder Lane, talented author and writer—has found the fountain of youth in the Ozark hills. We may well believe that she has a "cheerful disposition" as her friend asserts.

"I was a regular little tomboy," Mrs. Wilder confesses, "and it was fun to walk the two miles to school." The folks were living in Minnesota then, but it was not long until Father Ingalls, who seems to have had a penchant for moving about, had located in Dakota. It was at De Smet, South Dakota, that Laura Ingalls, then eighteen years old, married A. J. Wilder, a farmer boy.

"Our daughter, Rose Wilder Lane, was born on the farm," Mrs. Wilder informs us, "and it was there I learned to do all kinds of farm work with machinery. I have ridden the binder, driving six horses. And I could ride. I do not wish to appear conceited, but I broke my own ponies to ride. Of course, they were not bad, but they were broncos." Mrs. Wilder had the spirit that brought success to the pioneers.

Mr. Wilder's health failed and the Wilders went to Florida. "I was something of a curiosity, being the only 'Yankee girl' the inhabitants ever had seen," Mrs. Wilder relates. The low altitude did not agree with Mrs. Wilder, though, and she became ill. It was then that they came to Rocky Ridge Farm near Mansfield, Wright County [Mo.], and there they have lived for twenty-five years.

Only forty acres was purchased, and the land was all timber except a four-acre, worn-out field. "Illness and traveling expenses had taken our surplus cash, and we lacked $150 of paying for the forty acres," Mrs. Wilder writes. "Mr. Wilder was unable to do a full day's work. The garden, my hens, and the wood I helped saw and which we sold in town took us through the first year. It was then I became an expert at the end of a cross-cut saw, and I still can 'make a hand' in an emergency. Mr. Wilder says he would rather have me help than any man he ever sawed with. And, believe me, I learned how to take care of hens and to make them lay."

Intelligent industry brings its own reward. Mr. and Mrs. Wilder not only paid for the forty acres, but they have added sixty acres more, stocked the farm to capacity, and improved it and built a beautiful modern home. "Everything sold by the Wilders brings a good price," their neighbor tells me, "because it is standard goods. It was by following strict business methods that they were enabled to build their beautiful home. Most of the material used was found on the farm. Fortunate indeed are those who are entertained at Rocky Ridge."

One may wonder that so busy a person, as Mrs. Wilder has proved to be, can find time to write. "I always have been a busy person," she says, "doing my own housework, helping the Man of the Place when help could not be obtained; but I love to work. And it is a pleasure to write. And, oh, I do just love to play! The days never have been long enough to do the things I would like to do. Every year has held more of interest than the year before." Folks who possess that kind of spirit get a lot of joy out of life as they travel the long road.

JOINED THE FAMILY IN 1911

Mrs. Wilder has held numerous important offices, and her stories about farm life and farm folks have appeared in the best farm papers. Her first article printed [for us] appeared in February 1911. It was a copy of an address prepared for *Farmer's Week*. So for seven years she has been talking to

Missouri women through these columns, talk that always has carried inspiration and incentive for worthwhile work.

Reading Mrs. Wilder's contributions, most folks doubtless have decided that she is a college graduate. But "my education has been what a girl would get on the frontier," she informs us. "I never graduated from anything and only attended high school two terms."

Folks who know Mrs. Wilder, though, know that she is a cultured, well-educated gentlewoman. Combined with inherent ability, unceasing study of books has provided the necessary education, and greater things have been learned from the study of life itself.

As has been asserted before, Mrs. Wilder writes well for farm folks because she knows them. The Wilders can be found ready to enter wholeheartedly into any movement for community betterment, and the home folks are proud of the reputation that Mrs. Wilder has established. They know that she has won recognition as a writer and state leader because of ability alone.

The Old Dash Churn
SEPTEMBER 1916

All the world is queer, except for thee and me," said the old Quaker to his wife, "and sometimes I think thee is a little queer."

The Man of the Place once bought me a patent churn. "Now," said he, "throw away that old dash churn. This churn will bring the butter in three minutes." It was very kind of him. He had bought the churn to please me and to lighten my work, but I looked upon it with a little suspicion.

There was only one handle to turn and opposite it was a place to attach the power from a small engine. We had no engine so the churning must needs be done with

"I wish you would bring in my old dash churn," I said to the Man of the Place. "I believe it is easier to use than this after all."

one hand, while the other steadied the churn and held it down. It was hard to do, but the butter did come quickly; and I would have used it anyway because the Man of the Place had been so kind.

The tin paddles which worked the cream were sharp on the edges, and they were attached to the shaft by a screw which was supposed to be loosened to remove the paddles for washing; but I could never loosen it and usually cut my hands on the sharp tin. However, I used the new churn, one hand holding it down to the floor with grim resolution, while the other turned the handle with the strength of despair as the cream thickened. Finally, it seemed that I could use it no longer. "I wish you would bring in my old dash churn," I said to the Man of the Place. "I believe it is easier to use than this after all."

"Oh!" said he. "You can churn in three minutes with this, and the old one takes half a day. Put one end of a board on the churn and the other on a chair and sit on the board, then you can hold the churn down easily!" And so when I churned I sat on a board in the correct mode for horseback riding and though the churn bucked some, I managed to hold my seat.

"I wish," said I to the Man of the Place, "you would bring in my old dash churn." (It was where I could not get to it.) "I cut my hands on these paddles every time I wash them."

"Oh, pshaw!" said he. "You can churn with this churn in three minutes—"

One day when the churn had been particularly annoying and had cut my hand badly, I took the mechanism of the churn—handle, shaft, wheels, and paddles all attached—to the side door which is quite high from the ground and threw it as far as I could. It struck on the handle, rebounded, landed on the paddles, crumpled, and lay still—and I went out and kicked it before I picked it up. The handle was broken off, the shaft was bent, and the paddles were a wreck.

"I wish," I remarked casually to the Man of the Place, "that you would bring in my old dash churn. I want to churn this morning."

"Oh, use the churn you have," said he. "You can churn in three minutes with it. What's the use to spend half a day—"

"I can't," I interrupted. "It's broken."

"Why, how did that happen?" he asked.

"I dropped it—just as far as I could," I answered in a small voice, and he replied regretfully, "I wish I had known that you did not want to use it. I would like to have the wheels and shaft, but they're ruined now."

෴

As the old Quaker remarked to his wife, "Sometimes I think thee is a little queer."

My Apple Orchard
JUNE 1912

by [Mrs.] A. J. Wilder*

When I bought my farm in the fall, some years ago, there were eight hundred apple trees on it growing in nursery

---

*Although by-lined simply A. J. Wilder, what existing manuscript evidence there is of Almanzo's writing strongly suggests to scholars that Laura did all of the for-publication work in her household.

rows. Two hundred had been set out the spring before, in an old worn-out field, where the land was so poor it would not raise a stalk of corn over four feet high. This field was all the land cleared on the place; the rest of the farm was covered with oak timber.

Almanzo by one of his many fine apple trees

I have always thought it must have been a good agent who persuaded the man of whom I bought the place to mortgage it for one thousand apple trees when the ground was not even cleared on which to set them. However, he unloaded his blunder onto me, and I knew nothing about an orchard; did not even know one apple from another. I did know though that apple trees, or indeed trees of any kind, could not be expected to thrive in land too poor to raise corn fodder, so whenever I made a trip to town, I brought back a load of wood ashes from the mill or a load of manure from the livery barn and put it around those trees that were already set out in the field.

> The land was so poor it would not raise a stalk of corn over four feet high.

I cleared enough land that winter on which to set out the trees from the nursery, broke it the next spring, and put in the trees after I had worked it as smooth as I could. The trees already set out were twenty-five feet apart in the rows and thirty-two feet between the rows, so I set the others the same way. I dug the holes for the trees large and deep, making the dirt fine in the bottom and mixing some wood ashes with it.

I handled the trees very carefully so as not to injure the roots and spread the roots out as nearly as possible in a natural manner when setting the trees. Fine dirt was put over the roots at first and pressed down firmly; then the dirt was shoveled in to fill the hole. Some more wood ashes were mixed with the dirt when it was being shoveled in. I did not hill the dirt up around the tree but left it a little cupping for conserving moisture. All trash was raked away, leaving it clean and smooth, and again I used some wood ashes, scattering them around the tree, but being careful that none touched it to injure the bark. The ashes were used altogether with the idea of fertilizing the soil and with no idea of any other benefit, but I think they may have saved my orchard.

It is confessing to a colossal ignorance, but I found out later that I planted woolly aphids on nearly every one of my apple tree roots. At the time, I thought that for some reason they were a little moldy. I read afterward in an orchard paper that the lye from wood ashes would destroy the woolly aphids and save the tree; and as the use of wood ashes around the trees was kept up for several years, I give them the credit for saving my trees.

As I never allowed hunting on the farm, the quail were thick in the orchard and used to wallow and dust themselves like chickens in this fine dirt close to the tree. I wish this fact to be particularly noted in connection with the other fact that I had no borers in my trees for years.

A near neighbor set out two thousand trees about the same time and lost seven-eighths of them because of borers. He used every possible means to rid his trees of them except the simple one of letting the quail and other birds live in his orchard. Instead, he allowed his boys to kill every bird they saw.

My apples were sound and smooth, not wormy, which

I also credit to the birds for catching insects of all kinds as I never sprayed the trees. Within the last few years, the hunters, both boys and men, have been so active that it has been impossible to save my quail; and so I have had to begin the eternal round of spraying and cutting the trees to get the borers out.

When I set the trees, I trimmed them back a good deal. While I knew nothing of the science of trimming, I knew that I did not want a forked tree, so I trimmed to one stem with a few little branches left at the top. I watched the trees as they grew and trimmed away, while they were very small, all the branches that would interlock or rub against another branch.

In the fall I always whitewashed the trees to keep the rabbits from gnawing the bark, and if the storms washed it off, I whitewashed them again. Every spring they were whitewashed in April as a sort of house-cleaning and to make the bark smooth so it would not harbor insects, for I found that if there was a rough place, that was where the eggs of insects were deposited.

Between the trees, I raised corn, potatoes, and garden until the trees were eight years old, when I seeded that land down to timothy and clover. Of course, when I raised crops, I fertilized them enough to make them grow, and the trees always got their share. As a result, I get a good hay crop out of the orchard, making two good crops from the land.

I think that one thing that has made my orchard a success is that I took individual care of each tree. What that particular tree needed it got. Wife and I were so well acquainted with the trees that if I wished to mention one to her, I would say "that tree with the large branch to the south," or "the tree that leans to the north," etc. The tree that leaned was gently taught to stand straight so that the sun would not burn the bark. This was done by tying it to a stake firmly driven into the ground on the south side of the tree and from time to time shortening the string which held it.

The trees came into bearing at seven years old, and the apples were extra well-colored and smooth-skinned. I have had apple buyers and nursery men tell me that my orchard was the prettiest they ever saw, and my Ben Davis are different from any I have ever seen in being better colored and flavored and in the texture of the flesh. People even refuse to believe that they are Ben Davis at times. My orchard is mostly Ben Davis, and the rest is Missouri Pippin.

If I were to start another orchard, I would plow and cultivate the land for several seasons to prepare it for the trees. The wildness and roughness should be worked out in order to give the little trees a fair chance. Then I should plant apple seed where I wanted the trees to stand, and then bud onto the sprout the variety I wished to raise. In this way the taproot would not be disturbed,

as it is by moving the tree, but would run straight down. This makes a longer-lived, stronger tree.

On Chickens and Hawks
JUNE 1917

In the spring a young man's fancy lightly turns to thoughts of love," sings the poet, but in the spring the fancy of a hawk surely turns to spring chickens. Day after day, he dines on the plumpest and fairest of the flock. I may spend half the day watching and never catch a glimpse of him, then the moment my back is turned—*swoop!*—and he is gone with a chicken.

> I should like to sentence the ex-governor who vetoed the state bounty on hawks to make his living raising chickens.

I should like to sentence the ex-governor who vetoed the state bounty on hawks to make his living raising chickens in the hills and not permit him to have a gun on the place just by way of fitting the punishment to the crime.

I know it is said that hawks are a benefit to the farmers because they catch field mice and other pests, but I am sure they would not look for a mouse if there were a flock of chickens nearby.

THE PIONEER SPIRIT

"The days of wilderness adventure are not past! The pioneer spirit is not dead!"

Rocky Ridge Farm

JULY 1911

by [Mrs.] A. J. Wilder

To appreciate fully the reason why we named our place Rocky Ridge Farm, it should have been seen at the time of the christening. To begin with, it was not bottom land nor by any stretch of the imagination could it have been called second bottom. It was, and is, uncompromisingly ridge land, on the very tip-top of the ridge at that, within a very few miles of the highest point in the Ozarks. And rocky —it certainly was rocky when it was named, although strangers coming to the place now say, "But why do you call it Rocky Ridge?"

The place looked unpromising enough when we first saw it, not only one but several ridges rolling in every direction and covered with rocks and brush and timber. Perhaps it looked worse to me because I had just left the prairies of South Dakota where the land is easily farmed. I had been ordered south because those prairies had robbed me of my health,* and I was glad to leave them, for they had also robbed me of nearly everything I owned by continual crop failures. Still, coming from such a smooth country, the place looked so rough to me that I hesitated to buy it. But wife had taken a violent fancy to this particular piece of land, saying if she could not have it, she did not want any because it could be made into such a pretty place. It needed the eye of faith, however, to see that in time it could be made very beautiful.

> We bought Rocky Ridge Farm and went to work. We had to put a mortgage on it of $200, and had very little except our bare hands with which to pay it off, improve the farm, and make our living while we did it.

*Almanzo suffered a stroke after a bout with diptheria. He was left with a lifelong limp.

Kansas State Historical Society

Almanzo, center, knew that mules were best for Rocky Ridge travel

So we bought Rocky Ridge Farm and went to work. We had to put a mortgage on it of $200, and had very little except our bare hands with which to pay it off, improve the farm, and make our living while we did it. It speaks well for the farm, rough and rocky as it was, that my wife and myself with my broken health were able to do all this.

A flock of hens—by the way, there is no better place in the country for raising poultry than right here—a flock of hens and the wood we cleared from the land bought our groceries and clothing. The timber on the place also made rails to fence it and furnished the materials for a large log barn.

At the time I bought it there were on the place four acres cleared and a small log house with a fireplace and no windows. These were practically all the improvements, and there was not grass enough growing on the whole forty acres to keep a cow. The four acres cleared had been set out to apple trees, and enough trees to set twenty acres more were in nursery rows near the house. The land on which to set them was not even cleared of the timber. Luckily, I had bought the place before any serious damage had been done to the fine timber around the building site, although the start had been made to cut it down.

It was hard work and sometimes short rations at the first, but gradually the difficulties were overcome. Land was cleared and prepared by heroic effort in time to set out all the apple trees, and in a few years the orchard came into bearing. Fields were cleared and brought to a good state of fertility. The timber around the buildings was thinned out enough so that grass would grow between the trees, and each tree would grow in good shape, which has made a beautiful park of the grounds. The rocks have been picked up and grass seed sown so that the pastures and meadows are in fine condition and support quite a little herd of cows, for grass grows remarkably well on "Rocky Ridge" when the timber is cleared away to give it a chance. This good grass and clear spring water make it an ideal dairy farm.

Sixty acres more have been bought and paid for, which, added to the original forty, makes a farm of one hundred acres. There is no wasted land on the farm except a wood lot which we have decided to leave permanently for the timber. Perhaps we have not made so much money as farmers in a more level country, but neither have we been obliged to spend so much for expenses; and as the net profit is what counts at the end of the year, I am not afraid to compare the results for a term of years with farms of the same size in a more level country.

Our little Rocky Ridge Farm has supplied everything necessary for a good living and given us good interest on all the money invested every year since the first two. No year has it fallen below 10 percent, and one extra good year it paid 100 percent. Besides this, it has doubled in value and $3,000 more since it was bought.

We are not by any means through with making improvements on Rocky Ridge Farm. There are on the place five springs of running water which never fail even in the driest season. Some of these springs are so situated that by building a dam below them, a lake of three acres, twenty feet deep in places, will be near the house. Another small lake can be made in the same way in the duck pasture, and these are planned for the near future. But the first thing on the improvement program is building a cement tank as a reservoir around a spring which is higher than the buildings. Water from this tank will be piped down and supply water in the house and barn and in the poultry yards.

When I look around the farm now and see the smooth, green, rolling meadows and pastures, the good fields of corn and wheat and oats, when I see the orchard and strawberry field like huge bouquets in the spring or full of fruit later in the season, when I see the grapevines hanging full of luscious grapes, I can hardly bring back to my mind the rough, rocky, brushy, ugly place that we first called Rocky Ridge Farm. The name given it then serves to remind us of the battles we have fought and won and gives a touch of sentiment and an added value to the place.

In conclusion, I am going to quote from a little gift book which my wife sent out to a few friends last Christmas:

> "Just come and visit Rocky Ridge,
> Please grant us our request;
> We'll give you all a jolly time—
> Welcome the coming; speed the parting guest."

When Grandma Pioneered
AUGUST 1921

Grandma was minding the baby. "Oh, yes, she is sweet," she said, "but she is no rarity to me. You see, there were ten of us at home, and I was the oldest save one and that a boy. Seems like I've always had a baby to take care of. There were the little ones at home, then when I was older, I used to go help the neighbors at times; and there was always a new baby, for women them days didn't hire help unless they were down sick. When I was married, I had eleven of my own; now it's the grandchildren. No, indeed! Babies are no rarity to me! I was just a child myself when Father and Mother drove an ox team into the Ozarks. Father stopped the wagon in the thick woods by the big road, cut down some trees, and made a rough log cabin. But Mother never liked the house there; Father was away so much, and she didn't like to stay alone with the young ones so near the road. The Ozarks was a wild, rough country then, and all kinds of persons were passing; so Father built another house down by the spring out of sight, and we lived there.

> "Snakes were thick, too, and not so pleasant to meet; but none of us ever got bit, though we went barefoot all summer and until freezing weather."

"The woods were full of wild turkey and deer; when we children hunted the cows at night, we thought nothing of seeing droves of them. Snakes were thick, too, and not so pleasant to meet; but none of us ever got bit, though we went barefoot all summer and until freezing weather.

"Father used to tan the hides of deer and cattle and make our shoes, but later we had 'boughten' shoes. Then the men of the settlement would drive their ox teams south into the pineries in the fall and haul in logs to the mills. When they had hauled a certain number of loads, they were paid with a load of logs for themselves. These they had sawed into lumber and hauled the lumber to Springfield or Marshfield, seventy-five or one hundred miles, and sold it to get their tax money and shoes for the family.

"The men worked away a good deal and the mothers and children made the crops. Neighbors were few and far apart, but we were never lonely; didn't have time to be. We raised wheat and corn for our bread; hogs ran loose in the woods and, with venison and wild turkey, made our meat; we kept some sheep for the wool, and we raised cotton.

"After we had gathered the cotton from the fields, we handpicked it from the seeds. We carded the cotton and wool and then spun them into yarn and thread and wove them into cloth; we made our own blankets and coverlets and all the cloth we used, even our dresses.

"We worked long days. As soon as we could see in the morning, two of us would go into the woods and drive up the oxen for the day's work. Then we girls worked all day in the fields while Mother worked both in the house and out. Soon as supper was over, we built a brush fire in the fireplace to make light; and while one tended the fire to keep it bright, the others spun and wove and knit and sewed until ten or eleven o'clock. Passing a house after dark, anytime before midnight, you could always hear the wheel awhirring and the loom at work. We cooked in the fireplace, too, and I was sixteen years old before I ever saw a cookstove.

"When the crops were raised, Mother and we children did the threshing. The wheat was spread on poles with an old blanket under them to catch the grain as it dropped through; and we flailed it out with hickory poles, then blew the dust out in the wind, and it was ready to take to mill.

"We were taught to be saving. The shoes bought in the fall must last a year, and we were careful with them. When they got calico into the country, it cost twenty-five cents a yard, and if we had a calico dress we wore it for very best. When we took it off, we brushed off all the dust, turned it, folded it, and laid it carefully away.

"I never got much schooling. There was three months school in the year beginning the first Monday in September, but that was molasses-making, potato-digging, corn-picking time, and we older children had to stay home and do the work. The little ones went, and by the time they were older, we had things in better shape so they got lots more learning. But it was too late for us.

"Now school comes before the work at home, and when children go to school, it takes all their time; they can't do anything else.

"I wish folks now had to live for a little while like we did when I was young, so they would know what work is and learn to appreciate what they have. They have so much they are spoiled, yet every cent they get they must spend for something more. They want cars and pianos and silk dresses—Why, when I was married, all my wedding clothes were of my own spinning and weaving, but my husband was so proud he wouldn't let me wear my linsey dresses but bought me calico instead.

"Ah, well, times have changed! I'm an old woman and have worked hard all my life, but even now I can work down some of the young ones."

The Hard Winter
FEBRUARY 1917

In the late issue of a St. Louis paper, I find the following: "Experts in the office of home economics of the United States Department of Agriculture have found it is possible to grind whole wheat in an ordinary coffee mill fine enough for use as a breakfast cereal and even fine enough for use in breadmaking."

If the experts of the Department of Agriculture had asked any one of the two hundred people who spent the winter of 1880–81 in De Smet, South Dakota, they might have saved themselves the trouble of experimenting. I think, myself, that it is rather a joke on our experts at Washington to be thirty-six years behind times.

ahead of a hungry stove when the storm winds were blowing, but everyone took his turn good-naturedly. There is something in living close to the great elemental forces of nature that causes people to rise above small annoyances and discomforts.

A train got through May 10 and stopped at the station. All the men in town were down at the tracks to meet it, eager for supplies, for even the wheat had come to short rations. They found that what had been sent into the hungry town was a trainload of machinery. Luckily, there were also two emigrant cars well supplied with provisions which were taken out and divided among the people.

Our days of grinding wheat in the coffee mills were over, but we had learned without expert aid that it can be done and that the flour so ground will make good bread and mush. We had all become experts and demonstrated the fact.

Pioneering on an Ozark Farm

A Story of Folks Who Searched—and Found Health, Prosperity, and a Wild Frontier in the Mountains of Our Own State

JUNE 1921

The days of wilderness adventure are not past! The pioneer spirit is not dead!

We still have frontiers in our old, settled states where the joys of more primitive days may be experienced with some of their hardships and, now and then, a touch of their grim humor.

Nestled in a bend of the Gasconade River one and three-quarter miles south of Hartville, the county seat of Wright County, Missouri, is a little home which is gradually being made into a productive farm while losing none of its natural, woodland beauty. Its wild loveliness is being enhanced by the intelligent care it is receiving and by the determination of its owners to take advantage of, and work with, nature along the lines of her plans, instead of forcing her to change her ways and work according to man's ideals altogether—a happy cooperation with nature instead of a fight against her.

> The days of wilderness adventure are not past! The pioneer spirit is not dead!

Mr. and Mrs. Frink, owners and partners in the farm, come of pioneer stock and never were quite content with town and village life. They often talked of the joys of pioneering and dreamed of going to the western frontiers somewhere.

And the years slipped by, leaving their imprint: here and there a touch of snow in their dark hair, a few more lines around the eyes. Worst of all, they found their health breaking. Mrs. Frink's nerves were giving way under the constant strain of teaching music, and the combined efforts of each failed to pay the expenses of the many reverses, including doctor's bills with accompanying enforced idleness, and leave any surplus to be laid away for the old age that was bound to arrive with time.

THEN NATURE CALLED

All through the sweet days of spring and summer as Mrs. Frink sat hour after hour working with some dull music pupil, she heard the call of the big outdoors and would forget to count the beat as she dreamed of pioneering in some wild, free place, where, instead of hearing the false notes of beginners on the piano, she might listen to the music of the wild birds' song, the murmur of the wind among the treetops, and the rippling of some silver stream. And Mr. Frink fretted at the confinement of his law office and longed for wider spaces and the freedom of the old West he had known as a boy. But still they knew deep down in their hearts that there is no more frontier in the old sense.

By chance, Mr. Frink found the little nook, embraced by the bend of the river, tucked securely away in its hidden corner of the world, and Mrs. Frink said, "This is our frontier; we will pioneer here!"

There were only twenty-seven acres on the farm, mostly woodland, some flat, some set up edgeways, and the rest at many different angles as is the way of land in the Ozarks, where, as has been said, we can farm three sides of the land thus getting the use of many more acres than our title deeds call for.

I think at no time did Mr. and Mrs. Frink see the farm as it actually was, but instead they saw it with the eyes of faith as it should be later. What they bought were possibilities and the chance of working out their dreams. Mrs. Frink believed that here they could make their living and a little more. Mr. Frink was doubtful but eager to take a chance.

It required courage to make the venture, for the place was in a bad state. There were some six or seven acres of good bottom land in rather a poor state of cultivation and seven acres of second bottom, or bench land, on which was an old thrown-out, worn-out field. The rest was woodland, a system of brush thickets a rabbit could hardly penetrate. The valleys and glens were overgrown with grapevines and poison ivy, the abiding place of rattlesnakes and tarantulas. There were no fences worth the name.

The farm was bargained for in June, but negotiations were long and tedious, for it was necessary to bring three persons to the same mind at the same time; and it proved to be a case of many men of many minds instead. But at last the transaction was completed, and one sunny morning in August 1918, Mr. and Mrs. Frink gathered together their household goods and departed for the new home, on the frontier of the Ozarks, leaving Hartville without a mayor and its most prominent music teacher, with one closed law and insurance office.

They went in a dilapidated hack, containing household goods and a tent, drawn by a borrowed horse. Hitched at the back of the hack was Mat, the Jersey cow, and Bessie Lee, her nine-month-old calf. Dexter, a four-month-old colt, about twenty chickens, and three shoats had been sent ahead with a lumber wagon.

At four o'clock that afternoon the tent was pitched at Campriverside, and the Frinks were at home on their own farm. As Mr. Frink says, "The great problem was solved; we would not live our whole lives on a half-acre lot."

For supper they feasted on roasting ears and ripe tomatoes from their own fields. These were principal articles of fare for some time. The green corn later gave place to "grits," and finally these were replaced by their own grown corn meal.

The Frinks began their life on the farm in a small way and handicapped by debt. The price of the land was $600; but after paying off old indebtedness, there was left of their capital only $550 to pay for the land, build a house, and buy a horse. For there was no house on the land, and the tent must be the shelter until one could be built, while a horse was absolutely necessary to even a "one-horse farm."

Four hundred dollars was paid on the place and a note given for the balance of $200. Out of the remaining $150 a cabin was built and a horse bought. The material and labor on the house cost $120 and the horse cost $30.

> From the first, they lived from the proceeds of the little place.

Mr. and Mrs. Frink made up their minds at the start that the place must furnish fencing and building material as far as possible, and, really, log buildings seemed more in keeping with the rugged surroundings. The log house was built the first fall. It was fourteen by eighteen feet and a story and a half high. A shed for the stock, a chicken house, and a good many rods of fence have been added since to the improvements.

From the first, they lived from the proceeds of the little place. The land had been rented when bought, and they were to have the owner's share from the five acres of corn on the bottom field. In the fall, the renter put 125 bushels of good, hard, white corn in the hastily constructed crib. The crop could have been cashed for $300.

The next fall there were 100 bushels of corn as their share from the rented field and a bunch of hogs raised on the place were sold for $125.

In fifteen months after moving on the place, the note

for $200 and an old bill of $60 was paid off and a cream separator had been bought and paid for.

For the year of 1920 their share of corn was again 100 bushels, but because of the drop in prices, only $70 worth of hogs were sold. The income from cream and eggs averaged a little over a dollar a day for ten months of the year. And from the little new-seeded meadow, two tons of clover hay were cut and stacked.

The stock has been increased. There are now at home on the place three good Jersey cows, a team of horses, two purebred Poland China brood sows, ten shoats, and fifty laying hens.

There are also on hand six hundred pounds of dressed meat and stores of fruits and vegetables—the bulk of a year's provisions ahead. And best of all there are no debts but instead a comfortable bank account.

The expense of running the farm has been very little— about $25 a year for help. It is the intention that the eggs and cream shall provide money for running expenses, which so far they have done, leaving clear what money comes from selling the hogs, calves, and surplus chickens.

~

The start in raising chickens was made under difficulties. Mrs. Frink was eager to begin stocking the place, and early in the spring, when first the bargain was made for the farm, she wished to raise some chickens to take to it. At that time, the law forbade selling hens, so she borrowed one from a neighbor and set her. And that hen hatched out eleven roosters and only two pullets! Rather a discouraging start in the poultry business. But Mrs. Frink, while seeing the humor of the situation, refused to admit failure. She took the thirteen chickens out to the farm and put their coop up in a hickory tree beside the road. The roosters were fine large Orpingtons and attracted the attention and admiration of the neighbors.

Mrs. Frink refused to sell but offered to exchange for pullets and soon had a flock of twelve pullets and one rooster in the hickory tree. The pullets began laying in November, laid well all winter, and raised a nice bunch of chicks in the spring.

The plans of these Ozark pioneers are not yet completed. Thirteen acres of the woodland are being cleared and seeded to timothy and clover. In the woods pasture, the timber is being thinned, underbrush cleaned out, and orchard grass, bluegrass, and timothy are being sown.

Mr. Frink says, "There is much yet to be done. When the place is all cleared and in pasture, it will support six cows, which means from $50 to $60 a month for cream, and the fields in the bottom and on the bench will furnish grain for them and the hogs and chickens."

THREE

THE ROAD TO PROGRESS

"The more the farm is studied . . .
the more interesting it becomes."

The March of Progress

There is a movement in the United States today, wide-spread and very far-reaching in its consequences. People are seeking after a freer, healthier, happier life.

A great many of these people are discouraged by the amount of capital required to buy a farm and hesitate at the thought of undertaking a new business. But there is no need to buy a large farm. A small farm will bring in a good living with less work and worry, and the business is not hard to learn.

In a settlement of small farms the social life can be

> Keep up with the march of progress, for the time is coming when the cities will be the workshops of the world and abandoned to the workers, while real cultural, social, and intellectual life will be in the country.

much pleasanter than on large farms where the distance to the nearest neighbor is so great. Fifteen or twenty families on five-acre farms will be near enough together to have pleasant social gatherings in the evenings. The women can have their embroidery clubs, their reading clubs, and even the children can have their little parties without much trouble or loss of time. This could not be done if each family lived on a 100- or 200-acre farm. There is less hired help required on the small farm also, and this makes the work in the house lighter.

I am an advocate of the small farm, and I want to tell you how an ideal home can be made on, and a good living made from, five acres of land.

Whenever a woman's homemaking is spoken of, the man in the case is presupposed, and the woman's homemaking is expected to consist in keeping the house clean and in serving good meals on time, etc. In short, that all of her homemaking should be inside the house. It takes more than the inside of the house to make a pleasant home, and women are capable of making the whole home, outside and in, if necessary. She can do so to perfection on a five-acre farm by hiring some of the outside work done.

However, our ideal home should be made by a man and a woman together. First, I want to say that a five-acre farm is large enough for the support of a family.* From $75 to $150 a month, besides a great part of the living, can be made on that size farm from poultry or fruit or a combination of poultry, fruit, and dairy.

This has been proved by actual experience so that the financial part of this small home is provided for.

Conditions have changed so much in the country within the last few years that we country women have no need to envy our sisters in the city. We women on the farm no longer expect to work as our grandmothers did.

With the high prices to be had for all kinds of timber and wood, we now do not have to burn wood to save the expense of fuel, but can have our oil stove, which makes the work so much cooler in the summer, so much lighter and cleaner. There need be no carrying in of wood and carrying out of ashes, with the attendant dirt, dust, and disorder.

Our cream separator saves us hours formerly spent in setting and skimming milk and washing pans, besides saving the large amount of cream that was lost in the old way.

---

*Actually, their own farm was 100 acres at this time.

Then there is the gasoline engine. Bless it! Besides doing the work of a hired man outside, it can be made to do the pumping of the water and the churning, turn the washing machine, and even run the sewing machine.*

On many farms, running water can be supplied in the house from springs by means of rams or air pumps, and I know of two places where water is piped into and through the house from springs farther up on the hills. This water is brought down by gravity alone, and the only expense is the piping. There are many such places in the Ozark hills waiting to be taken advantage of.

This, you see, supplies water works for the kitchen and bathroom simply for the initial cost of putting in the pipes. In one farm home I know, where there are no springs to pipe the water from, there is a deep well and a pump just outside the kitchen door. From this, a pipe runs into a tank in the kitchen and from this tank there are two pipes. One runs into the cellar and the other underground to a tank in the barnyard, which is of course much lower than the one in the kitchen.

When water is wanted down cellar to keep the cream and butter cool, a cork is pulled from the cellar pipe by means of a little chain and, by simply pumping the pump

---

*Gas fumes and the possibility of fire seemed of less concern during the era of newly developed labor-saving devices than did any problems they might solve.

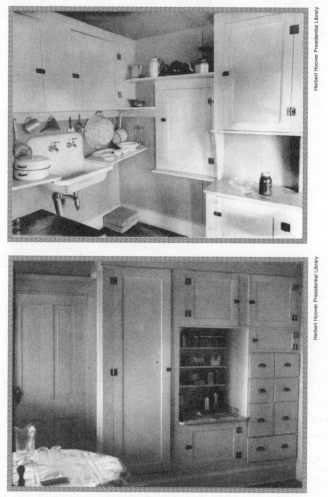

Mrs. Wilder's modern Ozark kitchen and dining room

outdoors, cold water runs into the vat in the cellar. The water already there rises and runs out at the overflow pipe through the cellar and out at the cellar drain.

When the stock at the barn need watering, the cork is pulled from the other pipe, and the water flows from the tank in the kitchen into the tank in the yard. And always the tank in the kitchen is full of fresh, cold water, because this other water all runs through it. This is a simple, inexpensive contrivance for use on a place where there is no running water.

It used to be that the woman on a farm was isolated and behind the times. A weekly paper was what the farmer read, and he had to go to town to get that. All this is changed. Now the rural delivery brings us our daily papers, and we keep up on the news of the world as well as or better than those who live in the city. The telephone gives us connection with the outside world at all times, and we know what is going on in our nearest town by many a pleasant chat with our friends there.

Circulating libraries, thanks to our state university, are scattered throughout the rural districts, and we are eagerly taking advantage of them.

The interurban trolley lines being built throughout our country will make it increasingly easy for us to run into town for an afternoon's shopping or any other pleasure. These trolley lines are, and more will be, operated by electricity furnished by our swift running streams; and in a few years our country homes will be lighted by this same electric power.

Yes, indeed, things have changed in the country, and we have the advantages of city life if we care to take them. Besides, we have what it is impossible for the woman in the city to have. We have a whole five acres for our backyard and all outdoors for our conservatory, filled not only with beautiful flowers, but with grand old trees as well, with running water and beautiful birds, with sunshine and fresh air, and all wild, free, beautiful things.

The children, instead of playing with other children in some street or alley, can go make friends with the birds on their nests in the bushes, as my little girl used to, until the birds are so tame, they will not fly at their approach. They can gather berries in the garden and nuts in the woods and grow strong and healthy, with rosy cheeks and bright eyes. This little farm home is a delightful place for friends to come for afternoon tea under the trees. There is room for a tennis court for the young people. There are skating parties in the winter; and the sewing and reading clubs of the nearby towns, as well as the neighbor women, are always anxious for an invitation to hold their meetings there.

In conclusion, I must say if there are any country women who are wasting their time envying their sisters in the city—don't do it. Such an attitude is out-of-date. Wake up to your opportunities. Look your place over, and if you have not kept up with the modern improvements and conveniences in your home, bring yourself up to date. Then take the time saved from bringing water from the spring, setting the milk in the old way, and churning by hand to build yourself a better social life. If you don't take a daily paper, subscribe to one. They are not expensive and are well worth the price in the brightening they will give your mind, and in the pleasant evenings you can have reading and discussing the news of the world.

Take advantage of the circulating library. Make your little farm home noted for its hospitality and the social times you have there. Keep up with the march of progress, for the time is coming when the cities will be the workshops of the world and abandoned to the workers, while real cultural, social, and intellectual life will be in the country.

Shorter Hours for the Farm Home Manager
JUNE 1913

When so much is being done to better the condition of the laboring man all over the world, it is good to know that the work of farm women is receiving its share of attention. Thinking persons realize that the woman on the farm is a most important factor in the success or failure of the whole farm business, and that, aside from any kindly feeling toward her, it pays in dollars and cents to conserve her health and strength. Women on the farm have not, as a rule, the conveniences that city housekeepers have; and their work includes much outside work, such as gardening, caring for chickens, and gathering as well as putting up fruits and vegetables.

Farm women have been patient and worked very hard. It has seemed sometimes as though they and their work were overlooked in the march of progress. Yet improvement has found them out, and a great many helps in their work have been put into use in the last few years. Farm homes with modern heating, lighting, and water equipment are increasing in number, and although the majority have not yet advanced so far as that, a great number have passed the stage of the bucket brigade from the spring or the hand over hand hauling of water from deep wells. It is getting to be quite the common thing to have the water piped down from the spring with a ram, or forced up from the bottom of deep wells by the compressed air pump. So, many steps have been saved the women folks, for they did most of the water carrying. It

> It has seemed sometimes as though they and their work were overlooked in the march of progress.

is so much easier to turn a faucet when one wants a bucket of water; and the time and strength saved can be used to so much better advantage in other ways.

Cream separators are taking the place of the troublesome setting of milk; gardens are being planted in rows so that a horse will do in a few minutes what would be a work of hours by hand; home canning outfits are lessening the labor of canning fruits and vegetables; kitchen cabinets are saving steps in the kitchen; and bread and cake mixers save tired hands and arms. Just the change from heavy ironware utensils to graniteware and tin has made more difference than one would think at first.

Vacuum cleaners have almost done away with housecleaning time for many farm women. In place of the above-ground cellar there is the simple little hanging cellarette. Several shelves of convenient size, either round or square, are fastened together the required distance apart. A close-fitting case or cover of two thicknesses of burlap or bran sack is made which completely encloses all the shelves and is closely buttoned down one side for the door. The "cellar" is then hung from the ceiling in some convenient place; a leaky bucket full of water is hung above it so that the water will drip on it, keeping all the burlap wet; a pan is set under it to catch the drips—and there you have a handy cellar for keeping cool the butter and the milk. One will save many a trip up and down cellar stairs or perhaps down to the spring. This hanging cellar is kept cool by the evaporation of the water from its surface.

A friend of mine was unable to stand the heat of the cookstove in summer, so she bought an inexpensive oil stove and a fireless cooker. Anything which required long cooking she started on the oil stove, then placed in the fireless cooker, finishing off, if necessary, when the time came by a few minutes browning on the oil stove. The combination worked perfectly. There was only a little heat from the oil stove and none at all from the fireless cooker. There was none of the labor of carrying in fuel and keeping up fires and of taking up ashes; and the cleaning up of the dust and dirt was all saved, and there was no increase in the running expenses, for the wood on the farm sold and bought the coal oil for the oil stove.

Another labor-saving idea is the use of a small work-table on casters, which can be easily moved from place to place. If cupboards, stove, and table are some distance apart, this is a great step saver. At one trip it can take from the cupboard to the stove all the things necessary in the getting of a meal. The meal can be dished up on it, and all taken to the dining table at once. The dishes can be taken away to wash upon it.

It was while recovering from a serious illness that I discovered the uses and value of a high stool. It is surprising how much of the housework can be done while sitting— ironing, washing dishes, preparing vegetables and dishes to cook or bake and even such cooking as frying griddle cakes can be accomplished while sitting. There should be a footrest on the stool so the feet will not hang, and it should be light so it can be easily moved. The movable table and the high stool form a combination for saving steps and tiresome standing that is hard to beat.

Ideas for using the things at hand to make our work easier will come to us if we notice a little. For instance, if we keep some old newspapers on hand in the kitchen, the uses we find for them will multiply. Rub the stove over with one when washing the dishes, and the disagreeable task of blacking the stove can be delayed much longer. The paper can be burned and our hands remain clean. Put papers on the worktable to set the pots and pans on while working, and the table will not have to be scoured. When the men come to a meal with their work clothes on from some particularly dirty job, newspapers spread over the tablecloth will save a hard job of washing and ironing.

> The more the farm is studied . . . the more interesting it becomes

Time and strength saved by the use of one help make it easier to get the next, and the time saved gives leisure to meet with the neighbors and find still other ways of doing the work more easily. Talking things over is a great help as is also the planning of the work so that the whole family can work together to advantage and without friction. As in any other business each one must do his work well and on time so as not to hinder the others in what they are trying to accomplish.

〰

It takes careful thought and planning to have the household machinery run smoothly and to the minute, with meals on time so that the farm work will not be hindered; and the woman who can do this and the outside work connected with the house has proven her executive ability and business talent.

While system is a great help in the work, it is best to get a new light on it once in a while, so we will not get in a rut and do things a certain way because we are in the habit, when we might make some improvement. It helps in finding the little kinks that need straightening out in our work, to notice if there is any of it that we dread to do, and if there is, then study that thing and find some way to do it differently. Perhaps just some little change will be a great help. A woman's work on the farm is very interesting if thought and study are given it, and in no other business can a woman so well keep up with her husband in his work. The more the farm is studied with the help of good farm papers and the Experiment Stations, the more interesting it becomes; and the woman on a farm may, if she wishes, become such an expert as to take the place of a farm advisor. Work in which we are interested can never become drudgery so long as we keep up that interest.

One thing is most important if we expect to keep rested and fit to do our best, and that is not to worry over the work nor to try to do it before the time comes. The feeling of worry and strain caused by trying to carry the whole week's work at once is very tiring. It doesn't pay to be like the woman of years ago in old Vermont who opened the stairway door at five o'clock on Monday morning and called to the hired girl: "Liza! Liza! Hurry up and come down! Today is wash day and the washing not started; tomorrow is ironing day and the ironing not begun; and the next day is Wednesday and here's the week half gone and nothing done yet."

Better for a little while each day to be like the tramp who was not at all afraid of work, yet could lie down right beside it and go to sleep. Slipping away to some quiet place to lie down and relax for fifteen minutes each day, if no longer, rests both mind and body surprisingly. This rest does more good if taken at a regular time, and the work goes along so much better when we are rested and bright that there is no time lost.

Change is rest! How often we have proved this by going away from our work for a day or even part of a day, thinking of other things and forgetting the daily round for a little while. On coming back, the work is taken up with new interest and seems much easier.

If it is not possible to go away, why not let the mind wander a little when the hands can do the task without our strict attention? I have always found that I did not get so tired, and my day seemed shorter when I listened to the birds singing or noticed from the window the beauties of the trees or clouds. This is a part of the farm equipment that cannot be improved upon, though it might be increased with advantage. Perhaps someday we will all have kitchens like the club kitchen lately installed in New York where everything from peeling the potatoes to cooking the dinner and washing the dishes is done by electricity, but the birds' songs will never be any sweeter nor the beauties of field and forest, of cloud and stream, be any more full of delight, and these are already ours.

We Revel in Water!
APRIL 1916

There once was a farmer, so the story goes, who hauled water in barrels from a distant creek. A neighbor remonstrated with him for not digging a well and having his water supply handier. The farmer contended that he did not have time.

"But," said the neighbor, "the time you would save by

not having to haul water would be more than enough to do the work."

"Yes, I know," replied the farmer, "but you see, I am so busy hauling water that I can't get time to dig the well."

There is a story of another man who also had trouble in supplying his place with water. This man hauled water for half a mile.

"Why don't you dig a well," asked a stranger, "and not haul water so far?" "Well," said the farmer, "it's about as fur to water one way as 'tis t'other."

I do not pretend to be the original discoverer of these stories, neither do I vouch for their truthfulness, but I do know that they correctly picture the fix we were in before we moved the spring.

> "I am so busy hauling water that I can't get time to dig the well."

We "packed water from the spring" for years at Rocky Ridge Farm. Now and then, when we were tired or in a special hurry, we would declare that something must be done about it. We would dig a well or build a cistern or something, the "something" being rather vague. At last the "something" was what we did. Like the men in the stories, we were too busy "packing water" to dig a well, and anyway it was "about as fur to water one way as t'other," so we decided to make an extra effort and move a spring. There were several never-failing springs on the farm, but none of them were right at the house. We did not wish to move the house, and besides it is very easy to move a spring, if one knows how, much easier than to move a house.

Our trouble was to decide which spring. The one from which we carried water was nearest, but it would require a ram to raise the water up to the house as the spring was in a gulch much lower than the buildings. Then, too, although it never went dry, it did run a little low during a dry spell. There were the three springs in the "Little Pasture." They ran strong enough, but they also would require a ram to lift the water. We wished our water supply to be permanent and as little trouble to us as possible when once arranged, so we looked further. Up on a hill in the pasture about 1,400 feet from the buildings was a spring which we had been watching for a year. The flow of water was steady, not seeming to be much affected by dry weather.

We found by using a level that this spring, at the head of a hollow in the hill, was enough higher than the hill where the buildings were situated to give the water a fall of sixty feet. We decided to move this spring, and the Man of the Place would do it with only common labor to help. The spring was dug out down to solid rock in the shape of a well, and a basin made in this a foot deep. In this well was built a cement reservoir eight feet in diameter, the walls of which were eleven feet high, extending three feet above the surface of the ground. It holds about thirty barrels of water. A heavy cement cover in the form of an arch was placed over the top. It takes two men to lift it so that no one will look in from curiosity and leave the cover displaced.

The cement was reinforced with heavy woven wire fence to make it strong. The walls and cover are so thick and the shade of the oaks, elms, and maples surrounding it so dense that the water does not freeze in winter and is kept cool in summer. A waste pipe was laid in the cement six inches from the top of the reservoir to allow the surplus water to flow off if the reservoir should become overfull. It is in the nature of a water trap as the opening is beneath the surface of the water and both ends are covered with fine screen to prevent anything from entering the pipe.

The pipe that brings the water down to the buildings is in the lower side of the reservoir about a foot from the bottom. It was laid in the cement when the wall was built so that it is firmly embedded. The end which projects into the water was fitted with a drive well point, screened to keep out foreign substances and prevent sand and gravel from washing into the pipe.

The pipe is laid two feet underground all the way to the buildings, and grass grows thickly over it for the whole distance. Because of this, the water does not become heated while passing through in warm weather, and there is no danger of its freezing and bursting the pipe in winter. The screen in the drive well point is brass, and the pipes are heavily galvanized inside and out. There is, therefore, no taste of iron or rust added to the water. We have moved the spring so that it flows into a corner of the kitchen as pure as at its source.

We have multiplied our spring as well as moved it. We revel in water! There is a hydrant in the hen house, one in the barn, one in the calf lot, one in the garden, and one at the back of the house besides the faucets in the house. The supply of water is ample, for we tried it thoroughly during a dry season. By attaching a hose to a hydrant, we can throw water over the top of the house or barn in a steady stream with the full force of a sixty-foot fall and thirty barrels of water behind, so we feel we have protection in case of fire.

A man came out from town one day, and after seeing the water works and drinking some of the water, he exclaimed, "Why, this is better than living in town!"

We have saved more than time enough to dig a well; but now we do not need to dig it, so we find that time seems to run in doubles this way as well as the other.

We are told that "There is no great loss without some small gain." Even so, I think that there is no great gain without a little loss. We do not carry water from the spring anymore, which is a very great gain, but it was sometimes pleasant to loiter by the way and that we miss a little.

FOUR

CHANGING TIMES
FOR WOMEN

*"Although still a vital part of a
woman's life, marriage is not now the
end and aim of her existence."*

The Home Beauty Parlor
APRIL 1914

Beauty is but skin deep" says the old adage, and most of us would be glad to know it was as deep as that. Why ugliness should have been made a virtue in the teaching of our youth is passing strange. We all admire beauty of character, but the possession of it is no excuse for neglecting our personal appearance. Indeed it seems to me there must be a fault in the character when one is satisfied with anything less than the best she can make of herself. It is not vanity to wish to appear pleasing to the eyes of our home folks and friends, nor is it a matter of small importance. To be well-groomed and good to look at will give us an added self-respect and a greater influence over others.

It is more difficult for country women than for those in the city to make a well-groomed appearance, for they usually do rougher work, and they cannot go to a beauty parlor and have themselves put in trim as the city woman can. However many barber shops there may be in a country town, there is almost never a beauty parlor for the women.

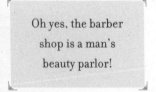

Oh yes, the barber shop is a man's beauty parlor!

(Oh yes, the barber shop is a man's beauty parlor! They have things put on their hair to prevent its falling out and to make it grow; they have soothing lotions and astringents and powder put on their faces. Don't let any of them tell you a beauty parlor is foolish or unnecessary or any of those things.)

Until we can make a change in things, and have our beauty parlor in town where we can have the same attention that men do at theirs, we must do these things for ourselves.

We can make a very good job of it, too, with some good, pure soap, a bottle of dioxogen* and some orange

_____

*Perhaps hydrogen peroxide?

wood sticks, a bottle of glycerine and rosewater, and a good toothbrush. With these aids, we can take care of our complexion, our hair, our hands, and our teeth, and with these in good condition, we shall have all the skin-deep beauty necessary for practical purposes; and this will help rather than hinder us in making a beautiful character.

There are a few simple things to remember in caring for the complexion. When washing the face it should first be thoroughly cleansed with warm water, using a good soap, then the soap should be well rinsed off with clear, warm water. The warm water opens the pores of the skin and, with the soap, thoroughly cleanses them; the clear, warm water rinses out the soap so it will not clog the pores. The face should then be well rinsed with cold water, the colder the better, to close the pores and tighten the skin to prevent flabbiness. Cold water is one of the best aids in keeping a good complexion if it is used in this way. It keeps the pores of the skin from becoming enlarged and brings the blood to the face, thus keeping up a good circulation in the minute blood vessels; and this makes the skin look fresh and youthful.

Cheap perfumed soaps are apt to be injurious to the skin and their use is risky. A good castile soap is always good and not expensive when bought a large bar at a time.

When washing the face, the skin should always be rubbed up and outward, because it is the gradual sagging down of the muscles of the face that causes wrinkles. You can satisfy yourself of this by a few experiments before a glass. A good cold cream rubbed into the skin just before the cold water is used, and then wiped lightly off with a soft cloth, will help to keep the wrinkles away and make the skin softer.

Face and hands should always be well dried after washing. If they are not, the skin will become rough. Keep the bottle of glycerine and rosewater close by the washpan, and after the hands are washed and dried, while they are still damp, rub a few drops of this over them. Do this as many times a day as the hands are washed, and they will keep soft and white.

Wrap a little cotton around the point of one of the little orange wood sticks, dip it into the bottle of dioxygen, and wipe out the dirt from under the fingernails.

Then take a little dry cotton on the stick and dry under them. This will do away with the annoying black line, for it cleanses and bleaches and does not make the nail rough, to catch more dirt, as a knife or scissors will when used to clean the nails.

There are many simple things in daily use on a farm that are splendid beautifiers. Washing in buttermilk will whiten the hands and face. Fresh strawberries rubbed on the skin will bleach it, and rhubarb or tomatoes will remove stains from the fingers. None of these things will do the least harm. Common table salt is one of the best tooth powders, and, with a good brush and water, will keep the teeth clean and white.

The hair should not be washed too often, for this will cause it to fall. Still, the scalp should be kept clean. Wearing a little dust cap over the hair while doing the work will help greatly in this, and such frequent washings will not be necessary.

When washing the hair, it is best to dissolve the soap in a little water, making a soft soap. Rub this into the hair with water until it lathers well, then wash it off. Repeat if necessary. When the hair is clean, rinse it well with clear warm water until the soap is all out, then pour some cold water over the scalp to close the pores of the skin. This will prevent taking cold and also act as a tonic to the scalp. The addition of a little baking soda to the water will lighten the hair and help to make it fluffy.

A tea made from common garden sage will darken the hair and help it grow.

This and That—a Neighborly Visit with Laura
FEBRUARY 1916

I wonder if Missouri farm women realize the value in dollars and cents of the work they do from day to day in raising farm products for the market? How many persons when reading the astonishing amount received in a year

> We are told that the life of a woman on a farm is narrow and that the monotony of it drives many farm women insane.

for Missouri poultry and eggs think of the fact that it is practically all produced by the women, and as a side-line at that! For, of course, a woman's real business is the keeping of the house and caring for the family. Not only the care of the poultry, but also the raising of garden products and small fruits is largely women's work; and in many instances the greater part of the labor of producing cream and butter also falls to women. The fact is that while there has been a good deal of discussion for and against women in business, farm women have always been businesswomen, and I have never heard a protest.

❧

I find that it adds greatly to the interest of life to keep careful accounts of the business of housekeeping with its sidelines of poultry and small fruits.

Especially do the account books add a spice when the Man of the Place gets angry because the hens get into the barn and scratch things around, or when the grain is getting low in the bins in the spring and he comes to you and says: "Those durn hens are eating their heads off!"

Then, if you can bring your little account book and show him that the feed for the hens cost so much, and the eggs and poultry sold brought so much, leaving a good little profit besides the eggs and poultry used in the house, he will feel better about things in general and especially the hens.

A woman I know kept for one year the accounts of the household and her own especial little extra work and surprised herself by finding that by her own efforts she had made a clear profit of $395 during the year, and this without neglecting in any way her household or home duties.

The total for household expenses and her own personal expenses for the same time was $122.29. There is after all, you see, some excuse for the man who told a friend he was going to be married. "Be married!" the friend exclaimed, in surprise. "Why, you can't make a living for yourself!" To which the first man replied, sulkily: "Well, it's a pity if she can't help a little."

My friend proved that she could "help a little." Her books made such a good showing that her husband asked her to keep books for the farm, and so she was promoted to the position of farm accountant (without salary).

Considering the amount of time, labor, and capital invested, the farm books did not balance out so well as her own, and she became interested in hunting the reason why. So now she has become a sort of farm advisor with whom her husband consults on all matters of farm business.

We are told that the life of a woman on a farm is narrow and that the monotony of it drives many farm women insane. That life on a farm as elsewhere is just what we make it, that much and no more, is being proved every day by women who, like this one, pick up a thread connecting farm life with the whole, great outside world.

In the study of soils, of crops, their origin and proper cultivation and rotation; in the study of the livestock on the place, their proper selection and care; with the care of her house and poultry, always looking for a shortcut in the work to gain time for some other interesting thing, there does not seem to be much chance for monotony to drive her insane.

∽

That "all work and no play makes Jack a dull boy" is very true, I think. It is just as dull for Jill as it is for Jack, and so they formed a "neighborhood crochet club" down in "Happy Hollow." The women met and learned the new crochet patterns and visited (?)—well, gossiped, then— as the men do when they go to town on Saturday and have so much business (?) to attend to that they cannot get home until late chore time.

By the way, did you ever think that as much good can be done by the right kind of gossip as harm by the unkind sort? The crochet club made a little playtime mixed with the work all summer until bad weather and the grippe interfered in the fall. Jill was not so dull, and plans are made for the club to meet again soon.

～

We do enjoy sitting around the fireplace in the evening and on stormy days in the winter.

When we planned our new house, we determined that we would build the fireplace first, and the rest of the house if we could afford it—not a grate, but a good old-fashioned fireplace that will burn a stick of wood as large as a man can carry. We have seen to it besides that there is a wood lot left on the farm to provide those sticks. So far we have escaped having the grippe while all the neighborhood has been suffering with it. We attribute our good fortune to this same big fireplace and the two open stairs in the house. The fresh air they furnish has been much cheaper as well as pleasanter to take than the doctor's medicine.

Some old-fashioned things like fresh air and sunshine are hard to beat. In our mad rush for progress and modern improvements, let's be sure we take along with us all the old-fashioned things worthwhile.

The magazines say that the spring fashions will return to the styles of our grandmothers, ruffles, pantalettes, ribbon armlets, and all. It will surely be delightful to have women's clothes soft and fluffy again, and we need not follow the freak styles, you know. There is a distinct advantage in choosing the rather moderate, quiet styles, for the up-to-the-minute freaks soon go out, and then they call attention to their out-of-dateness by their striking appearance, while others in equally as good of a style, but not so pronounced, will be a pleasure for more than one season.

New Day for Women
JUNE 1918

How long has it been since you have seen an old maid? Oh, of course, one sees unmarried women every day, but it has been a good many years since I have seen a real "old maid" or "maiden lady." Even the terms sound strange and lead one back and back into memories.

There were old maids when I was a girl. Later, some of the older girls protested against being called "old maids" and insisted on being called "bachelor girls." There was some controversy over the question of whether women should be given such a title, I remember, but not having any special interest in the subject, I lost sight of it and awakened later to the fact that both old maids and bachelor girls had disappeared, how or when I do not know. In their place are simply women, young women, older women (never old women), married and unmarried women, divorced women and widows, with the descriptive adjective in the background; but nowhere in the world, I think, are there any old maids.

As one considers the subject, it becomes plain that this one fact contains the whole story and explanation of the change in the world of women, the broadening and enriching of their lives. In the days when old maids flourished, the one important fact in a woman's life was whether or not she was married, and as soon as a girl child reached maturity, she was placed in one of two classes and labeled accordingly. She was either Mrs.——or else an old maid.

> Although still a vital part of a woman's life, marriage is not now the end and aim of her existence.

THE WORLD IS OPEN TO US

As women became more interested in other things; as the world opened up to them its storehouse of activities and absorbing interests; when the fact that a woman was a doctor, a lawyer, a farmer or what not; when her work in and for the world became of more importance to the world than her private life, the fact of whether or not she was married did not receive the emphasis that it formerly did. To be sure, everyone knows that a woman's most important work is still her children, but other interests enter so largely into her life today that she is not classified solely on the one count. Although still a vital part of a woman's life, marriage is not now the end and aim of her existence. There are in the world many, many other ambitions and occupations to take up her attention.

Herbert Hoover Presidential Library

Laura Ingalls Wilder, household editor for the Ruralist

Women are successful lumber dealers, livestock breeders, caterers, curators, bacteriologists, pageant managers, cable code experts, and besides have entered nearly every ordinary profession. They have learned and are learning the most advanced methods of farming and scientific dairy management while it has become no uncommon thing for a woman to manage an ordinary farm. The exigencies of the war have thrust women into many new occupations that otherwise they might not have undertaken for many years, if ever.

Thousands of them have become expert munitions makers and, while we all hope there will be no need for that trade when the present war is ended, still there will be use for the trained technical skill which these women workers have acquired.

Women are running trains; they are doing the work in factories; they are clerks, jurors, representatives in Congress, and farm help. By the time the war is over, most of the economic and industrial systems of the world will be in the hands of the women. Quite likely, too, they will have, through the ballot, the control of the political governments of the world.

If by an inconceivable turn of fate, Germany should conquer in the struggle now going on,* women will be held in control by the military power and without doubt

---

*World War I.

will be again restricted to the home and children according to the rule laid down by Emperor William defining their sphere of activity; but this we will not permit to be possible.

When the democratic nations are victorious and the world is ruled by the ballot instead of the cannon, there is scarcely a doubt but what women will be included in the universal suffrage. Already the franchise has been given to six million women in England. A suffrage amendment to the Constitution of the United States missed being brought before congress by only a few votes, and there is no doubt but that the women of the United States will soon have the ballot.

In Russia, when the revolution occurred, the women took the franchise with the men as a matter of course and without question. In France, the old idea that women should rule through their influence over men is still alive but growing feeble. More and more women and men are coming to stand together on terms of frankness and equality.

WOMEN SHALL RULE

Italy is far behind the other nations in the emancipation of its women; still the women of Italy have a great influence. It was the use of German propaganda among the Italian peasant women that weakened Italy and caused the late reverse there.

We all realize with aching hearts that there is a great slaughter of men on the battle fronts and with the sexes about equal over the world before the war, what will be the result when millions of men are killed? When at last the "Beast of Berlin" is safely caged and the soldiers of freedom return home to settle quietly down into civil life once more, the women are going to be largely in the majority over the world. With the ballot in their hands, they are going to be the rulers of a democratic world.

> Will we be wise and true and strong enough to use this power for the best, or will we be deceived through our ignorance or driven on the wrong way by storms of emotion or enthusiasm?

There is a great deal of speculation about the conditions that will prevail after the war. Nearly all writers and thinkers are looking for a new order, a sort of social and industrial revolution; and they all expect it to come through the returned soldiers. No one, so far as I have found, is giving a thought to the fact that in a free democratic world the power will be in the hands of the women who have stayed quietly at home working, sorrowing, and thinking.

Will we be wise and true and strong enough to use this power for the best, or will we be deceived through our ignorance or driven on the wrong way by storms of emotion or enthusiasm? We have been privileged to look on and criticize the way the world has been run. "A man-made world" we have called it now and then, implying that women would have done so much better in managing its affairs. The signs indicate that we are going to have a chance to remake it nearer to the heart's desire. I wish I might be sure that we would be equal to our opportunity.

I suggested this idea of the coming power of women to a liberal-minded man, a man who is strongly in favor of woman suffrage, and he replied: "The women are no more ready for such a responsibility than the people of Russia were; they are ignorant along the lines of government and too uncontrolled in their emotions."

I wonder if he is right? The majority vote in a Democratic league of nations will be a great power to hold in inexperienced hands, a great responsibility to rest upon the women of the world.

Women's Work?
APRIL 1919

Flaring headlines in the papers have announced that "women will fight to hold jobs," meaning the men's jobs which they took when the men went to war. What to do about the situation seems to be a very important question. One would think that there must have been a great number of women who were idle before the war. If not, one wonders what has become of the jobs they had. To paraphrase a more or less popular song—I Wonder Who's Holding Them Now?

With men by the thousands out of work and the unemployment situation growing so acute as to cause grave fears of attempted revolution, women by the hundreds are further complicating affairs by adding their numbers to the ranks of labor, employed, unemployed, or striking as the case may be.

> Will these women take up their old work and give the men a chance to go back. . . . The women say not.

We heard nothing of numbers of women who could not find work before the war. They were all busy apparently and fairly well satisfied. Who is doing the work they left to fill the places of men who went into the army, or is that work undone?

It would be interesting to know, and it seems strange that while statistics are being prepared and investigations made of every subject under the sun, no one has compiled the records of "The Jobs Women Left or Woman's Work Undone."

But however curious we may be about the past, we are

more vitally interested in the future. Will these women take up their old work and give the men a chance to go back to the places they will thus leave vacant? The women say not.

Other women, also, besides those who took men's jobs, have gone out of the places they filled in pre-war days, out into community and social work and government positions which were created by and because of the war. Will these women go back? And again we hear them answer, "Never! We never will go back!" All this is very well, but where are they going and with them all of us?

> We must advance logically, in order, and all together if the ground gained is to be held.

I think this query could most truthfully be answered by a slang expression, which, though perhaps not polished, is very apt: "We don't know where we're going, but we're on our way."

It makes our hearts thrill and our heads rise proudly to think that women were found capable and eager to do such important work in the crisis of war-time days. I think that never again will anyone have the courage to say that women could not run world affairs if necessary. Also, it is true that when men or women have advanced, they do not go back. History does not retrace its steps.

But this too is certain. We must advance logically, in

order, and all together if the ground gained is to be held. If what has hitherto been women's work in the world is simply left undone by them, there is no one else to take it up. If in their haste to do other, perhaps more showy things, their old and special work is neglected and only half done, there will be something seriously wrong with the world, for the commonplace home work of women is the very foundation upon which everything else rests.

So if we wish to go more into world affairs, to have the time to work at public work, we must arrange our old duties in some way so that it will be possible. We cannot leave things at loose ends, no good housemother can do that; and we have been good housekeepers so long that we have the habit of finishing our work up neatly.

Women in towns and villages have an advantage over farm women in being able to cooperate more easily. There is talk now of community kitchens for them from which hot meals may be sent out to the homes. They have, of course, the laundries and the bake shops already.

We farm women, at least farm mothers, have stayed on the job, our own job, during all the excitement. We could not be spared from it as we realized, so there is no question of our going back or not going back. We are still doing business at the old place, in kitchen and garden and poultry yard; and no one seems to be trying to take our job from us.

But we do not wish to be left too far behind our sisters in towns and cities. We are interested in social and world betterment, in religion and politics; we might even be glad to do some work as a sideline that would give us a change from the old routine. We would like to keep up, if anyone can keep up with these whirling times, and we must have more leisure from the treadmill if we are to do any of these things.

We must arrange our work differently in some way. Why not a laundry for a farm neighborhood and a bakery also, so situated that they will be easily accessible to a group of farms?

Perhaps if we study conditions of labor and the forward movements of the world as related to the farm, we may find some way of applying the best of them to our own use.

The Woman's Place
MARCH 1922

Reading of an agricultural conference in Washington, D.C., I was very much interested in the address of Mrs. Sewell of Indiana on the place of the farmer's wife in agriculture. She drew a pathetic picture, so much so as to bring tears to the eyes of the audience.

Now, I don't want any tears shed over my position, but

I've since been doing some thinking on the farm woman's place and wondering if she knows and has taken the place that rightfully belongs to her.

Every good farm woman is interested as much in the business part of farm life as she is in the housework, and there comes a time, after we have kept house for years, when the housekeeping is mostly mechanical, while the outside affairs are forever changing, adding variety and interest to life.

As soon as we can manage our household to give us the time, I think we should step out into this wider field, taking our place beside our husbands in the larger business of the farm. Cooperation and mutual help and understanding are the things that will make farm life what it should be.

> To a woman who has been an "auxiliary" until she is tired of the word, it seems like a start toward the promised land.

And so, in these days of women's clubs from which men are excluded, and men's clubs that permit women to be honorary members only, I'm glad to know [there is a club] whereby farm men and women work together on equal terms and with equal privileges. To a woman who has been an "auxiliary" until she is tired of the word, it seems like a start toward the promised land.

FIVE

THE VALUE OF WORK

"Sometimes, I fancy we do not always appreciate the value of work and how dry and flavorless life would be without it."

Farmers—Need More Wives?

JULY 1916

One of the neighbors needed some help in the hay harvest. Being too busy to go himself, he called a town friend by telephone and asked him, if possible, to send out someone to work through haying. Mansfield has made a beautiful shady park of the public square in the center of the town, and it is the gathering place for those who have idle time on their hands. Everyone enjoys it, the busy man with just a few idle minutes as well as the town loafers who, perhaps, have a few busy minutes now and then. It seemed like a good place to look for a man to help in the hay field, so here the obliging friend went.

"Any of you fellows want a job?" he asked of a group resting in the shade. "Yes," said one man. "I do." "Work on a farm?" asked the friend. "Yes, for I need a job," was the reply. "Can you go out in the morning?" was the next question. "How far out is it?" asked the man who needed a job. "Two miles and a half," he was told. "Can't do it!" he exclaimed, dropping back into the restful position from which he had been disturbed. "I wouldn't go that far from town to work for anybody."

The Man of the Place, inquiring in town for help, was told that it was not much use to look for it. "Jack was in the other day and begged with tears in his eyes for someone to come help him get in his hay, and he couldn't get anyone." Jack's place is only half a mile from town, so surely it could not be too far out; but to be sure the sun was shining rather warm in the hay field and the shade in the park

> Farmers are being urged to raise more food for world consumption, to till more acres, and also produce more to the acre. Their hands are quite full now, and it seems that about the only way they could procure more help would be to marry more wives.

was pleasanter. All of which reminds one of the tramp of whom Rose Wilder Lane tells in her *Soldiers of the Soil*. She met him, one of many, while on her walking tour through the state of California. After listening to his tale of woe, she asked him why he did not look for work on a farm. She was sure there must be a chance to find a job there, for the farmers were very short of help. To her suggestion, the tramp replied, "Who wants to work like a farmer anyway!"

No one seems to want to "work like a farmer," except the farmer's wife. Well! Perhaps she does not exactly *want* to, but from the way she goes about it, no one would suspect that she did not. In our neighborhood we are taking over more of the chores to give the men longer days in the field. We are milking the cows, turning the separator, feeding the calves and the pigs, and doing whatever else is possible, even going into the fields at times. Farmers are being urged to raise more food for world consumption, to till more acres, and also produce more to the acre. Their hands are quite full now, and it seems that about the only way they could procure more help would be to marry more wives.

A few days ago, I ran away from a thousand things waiting to be done and stole a little visit with a friend. And so I learned another way to cut across a corner and save work. Here it is, the way Mrs. Craig makes plum jelly. Cook the plums and strain out the juice; then to three cups of the boiling juice add four cups of sugar and stir until dissolved. Fill jelly glasses at once and set to one side. If the juice is fresh, it will be jelled in the morning; but if the juice is from canned plums, it takes longer and may have to set over until the next day, but it jells beautifully in the end.

About Work
FEBRUARY 1919

There is good in everything, we are told, if we will only look for it; and I have at last found the good in a hard spell of illness. It is the same good the Irishman found in whipping himself.

> Sometimes, I fancy we do not always appreciate the value of work and how dry and flavorless life would be without it.

"Why in the world are you doing that?" exclaimed the unexpected and astonished spectator.

"Because it feels so good when I stop," replied the Irishman with a grin. And this thing of being ill certainly does feel good when it stops. Why, even work looks good to a person who has been through such an enforced idleness, at least when strength is returning. Though I'll confess, if work crowds on me too soon, I am like the friend who was recovering from influenza rather more slowly than is usually the case.

"I eat all right and sleep all right," said he. "I even feel all right, but just the sight of a piece of work makes me tremble."

"That," said I, "is a terrible affliction, but I have known persons who suffer from it who never had the influenza."

But I'm sure we will all acknowledge that there is an advantage in having been ill if it makes us eager for work once more. Sometimes, I fancy we do not always appreciate the value of work and how dry and flavorless life would be without it.

If work were taken from us, we would lose rest also, for how could we rest unless we first became tired from working? Leisure would mean nothing to us for it would not be a prize to be won by effort and so would be valueless. Even play would lose its attraction for, if we played all the time, play would become tiresome; it would be nothing but work after all.

In that case, we would be at work again and perhaps a piece of actual work would become play to us. How topsy-turvy! But there is no cause for alarm. None of us is liable to be denied the pleasure of working, and that is good for us no one will deny. Man realized it soon after he was sentenced to "earn his bread by the sweat of his brow," and with his usual generosity he lost no time in letting his womankind in on a good thing.

Two Heads Are Better Than One
AUGUST 1919

We are going to be late getting the hay in from the west meadow. Can't you come and rake it for us?" said the Man of the Place.

I could and did; also I drove the team on the hay fork to fill the big barn, for such is the life of a farmer's wife during the busy season.

"The colt has sprained his ankle. Come pet him while I rub on some liniment, and while you are there, I wish you'd look at the red heifer's bag and see what you think best to do for that swelling on it."

And so I halter broke the colt while the Man of the Place bathed the lame ankle, and then we decided that the red heifer had been bee stung and bathed her udder with salt and water.

I have finally got the weakly calf into good growing condition and turned it out in the pasture with the others, for I am by way of being an understudy for the veterinarian.

"What would you raise next year on that land we cleared of brush down by the creek? The hay on it is too thin, and it must be broken up." This was the question for my consideration at the breakfast table, and my answer was, "Raise the same crop on that as you do on the remainder of the land on that side of the creek. One large

94

field is better than two small ones, and time is saved in working. Put it into the regular rotation with the rest."

Not that the Man of the Place would do as I said unless he agreed with me, but getting my ideas helps him to form his own opinions, and he knows that two heads are better at planning than one.

One of my neighbors is managing the farm this summer during the absence of her husband. She planted and cultivated and has attended to the harvesting and threshing and haying. She, with the children, cares for the horses and cows, the pigs and poultry. She buys and sells and hires and fires. In short, she does all the work and business that her husband would do if he were here and keeps up her own work besides.

> The farmer's wife must know her own business, which includes the greatest variety of trades and occupations ever combined in one all-around person.

A farmer, to be successful, must understand his machinery and be a sort of blacksmith. He must be a carpenter, a road builder, enough of a civil engineer to know how to handle the creeks and washouts on his farm. He must, of course, understand all about the care of the animals on the farm

in sickness and in health; he must know all about the raising of crops and handling of soils, the fighting of pests and
overcoming of weather conditions and, in addition, must
be a good businessman so that he shall not lose all the
fruits of his toil in the buying and selling end of the game.

Besides being a helper in all these things with brains—
and muscle if necessary—the farmer's wife must know her
own business, which includes the greatest variety of trades
and occupations ever combined in one all-around person.
Think of them! Cook, baker, seamstress, laundrywoman,
nurse, chambermaid, and nurse girl. She is a poultry
keeper, an expert in dairy work, a specialist in canning,
preserving, and pickling, and besides all else, she must
be the mother of the family and a smiling hostess.

Tired to Death with Work
MARCH 1920

You are tired to death with work," I read. "Work with a
little 'w' is killing the soul out of you. Work with a little
'w' always does that to men if they give it the whole
chance. If you don't mix some big 'W' work in with it,
then indeed your life will be disastrous, and your days
will be dead."

"What is it you mean by big 'W' work?" he asked. "Of
course, that's the work you love for the work's sake. It's

the work you do because you love the thing itself you're working for."

I closed the book. "That is plenty enough to think about for a while," I said to myself. "I don't want any more ideas mixed with that until I thresh it out well."

We are all doing a great deal of little "w" work, and it is necessary and right that we should. We must work for the pay or the profit that comes from it whether or not we love what we are working for, because we must live and lay by something for old age.

> If instead we devote ourselves, a part of our time, to work we love for itself, for what we are accomplishing, we grow stronger and more beautiful of soul.

But it is sadly true that giving all our time and thought and effort to personal gain will cause us to become selfish and small and mean. If instead we devote ourselves, a part of our time, to work we love for itself, for what we are accomplishing, we grow stronger and more beautiful of soul.

Perhaps we all have been too intent on our own financial gain. From firsthand experience as well as the printed news, it would appear that no one is excessively fond of the work he is, or has been, doing. Everyone is insisting on more money and less work or more profit and less return for it—little "w" work, all of it.

But there are encouraging signs in these somewhat discouraging times of grafters and grafting, of profits and profiteering, of distrust and suspicion, jealousy and strife. Sounds ugly, does it not? But those are the things to which our attention is called daily.

However, as I have said, there are hopeful signs. Only the other day a county officer refused a $900 raise in his salary because, he said, knowing the condition of the country as he did, he knew that the money was needed so much worse for other things.

> To work for the good of the community without full reward in money but because we love our fellows and long for the common betterment is work with a big "W," work that will keep our souls alive.

Although it was a stormy day when I read of this man, it seemed as though the sunshine was streaming over the world. A public official placing the welfare of the community before his private gain so far as to refuse more pay for his services is wonderfully encouraging to our hopes for our country. If there were enough of such public-spirited men, the difficulties which we are facing as a nation would soon disappear.

To work for the good of the community without full reward in money but because we love our fellows and long for the common betterment is work with a big "W," work that will keep our souls alive.

Then there is the owner of the apartment house in New York who did not raise the rent! When at last his tenants had a meeting and voted to pay more rent, he refused to accept it; but when they insisted, he took it and spent it all on improvements which made the tenants more comfortable.

There is also the young woman with the musical talent and the lovely singing voice, who uses it so freely for the pleasure and benefit of others; and the one who grows beautiful flowers because she loves them and delights in giving them away.

There is, after all, a great deal of work being done in the world for the love of the thing worked for, with no thought of selfishness; and the lives of such workers are fuller and richer for it.

SIX

THE THINGS THAT MATTER

"The real things of life that are the common possession of us all are of the greatest value."

A Day Off Now and Then

FEBRUARY 1914

Distances are long in the country, and although it is very pleasant to go and spend the day with a friend, it takes a good while to see many people in that way. Women who have been rather isolated all summer need to be enlivened by seeing people, the more the better. There is something brightening to the wits and cheering to the spirits in congenial crowds that is found in nothing else. Why not form a neighborhood club and combine the pleasure of going "a visiting" with the excitement of a little crowd and the joy of entertaining our friends all together when our turn comes? It is less trouble to entertain several at once than to entertain several times; besides, there is a great saving of time, and as the club meets at first one house and then another, the neighborhood visiting is done with less of work and worry and more of pleasure than in any other way.

NEEDED BY COUNTRY WOMEN

It used to be that only the women in town could have the advantages of women's clubs, but now the woman in the country can be just as cultured a club woman as though she lived in town. The neighborhood club can take up any line of work or study the members wish. Courses of reading can be obtained from the state university or the International Congress of Farm Women, and either organization will be glad to help with plans, advice, and instruction. Bits of fancy work or sewing may be taken to the meetings, and the latest stitch or the shortcut in plain sewing can be learned by all. Recipes may be exchanged, good stories told, songs sung, and jokes enjoyed.

The serving of some dainty refreshments would add to the pleasure of the afternoon and keep the social graces in good practice. Women in the country, as well as those in town, need these occasions to show what charming hostesses and pleasant guests they can be. If the men folks want to go along, by all means, let them do so. They might gather by themselves and discuss farm matters. They might even organize and have a little farmers' club of their own, if they have not done so already; then they would be even more willing to hitch up and drive to the meeting place.

NO TIRESOME MEETINGS

There are so many ways to vary the meetings and programs they need never become tiresome or dull. Now and then the meeting may be held in the evening and an entertainment given by home talent. Sometimes the club might go in a body to a lecture or some amusement in town or for a little excursion to the nearest city. A regular organization with the proper officers; a motto and membership badges will add to the interest, as will also being an auxiliary of some larger organization such as the International Congress of Farm Women.

> The long, bright days of summer, when we all long to go picnicking and fishing, offer simply a different form of entertainment and social life and should be enjoyed to the full.

Although the fall with its greater amount of leisure may be the best time to start a club of this kind, it need not be given up at the coming of spring. The long, bright days of summer, when we all long to go picnicking and fishing, offer simply a different form of entertainment and social life and should be enjoyed to the full. Perhaps the meetings might best be further apart while the rush of work is on, but a day off now and then will never be noticed in the work and will do the workers a world of good.

What Became of the Time We Saved?
APRIL 1917

A few days ago, with several others, I attended the meeting of a women's club in a neighboring town. We went in a motor car, taking less than an hour for the trip on which we used to spend three hours before the days of motor cars; but we did not arrive at the time appointed nor were we the latest comers by any means. Nearly everyone was late, and all seemed in a hurry. We hurried through the proceedings; we hurried in our friendly exchanges of conversation; we hurried away; and we hurried all the way home where we arrived late as usual.

> What became of the time the motor car saved us? Why was everyone late and in a hurry?

What became of the time the motor car saved us? Why was everyone late and in a hurry? I used to drive leisurely over to this town with a team, spend a pleasant afternoon, and reach home not much later than I did this time, and all with a sense of there being time enough, instead of a feeling of rush and hurry. We have so many machines and so many helps, in one way and another, to save time; and yet I wonder what we do with the time we save. Nobody seems to have any!

Neighbors and friends go less often to spend the day. Instead, they say, "We have been planning for so long to come and see you, but we haven't had time," and the answer will be: "Everyone makes the same complaint. People don't go visiting like they used to. There seems to be no time for anything." I have heard this conversation, with only slight variations, so many times that I should feel perfectly safe to wager that I should hear it anytime the subject might be started. We must have all the time there is, the same as always. We should have more, considering the timesaving, modern conveniences. What becomes of the time we save?

❧

If there were any way possible of adding a few hours to the day, they could be used handily right now; for this is surely the farm woman's busy time. The gardens, the spring sewing, the housecleaning more or less caused by the change from cold to warm weather, and all the young things on the place to be cared for call for agility, to say the least, if a day's work is to be done in a day.

Some people complain that farm life is monotonous. They surely never had experience of the infinite variety of tasks that come to a farm woman in the merry springtime! Why, the ingenuity, the quickness of brain, and the sleight of hand required to prevent a young calf from spilling its bucket of milk at feeding time, and the patience necessary to teach it to drink is a liberal education in itself, while the vagaries of a foolish sitting hen will relieve the monotony for the entire day!

So much of the work of the farm that we take as a matter of course is strange and interesting to a person who is not used to it. A man who has been in business in town for over twenty years is moving his family to the farm this spring and expects to be a farmer. The old order, you see, is reversed. Instead of retiring from a farm to town, he is retiring from town to a farm. I was really surprised, in talking with him, to find how many things there are for a beginner to learn.

How to Furnish a Home
NOVEMBER 1917

As someone has said, "Thoughts are things," and the atmosphere of every home depends on the kind of thoughts each member of that home is thinking.

I spent an afternoon a short time ago with a friend in

The front room with the open stairway in the background

The window-seat corner of the front room

her new home. The house was beautiful and well-furnished with new furniture, but it seemed bare and empty to me. I wondered why this was until I remembered my experience with my new house. I could not make the living room seem homelike. I would move the chairs here and there and change the pictures on the wall, but something was lacking. Nothing seemed to change the feeling of coldness and vacancy that displeased me whenever I entered the room.

Then, as I stood in the middle of the room one day wondering what I could possibly do to improve it, it came to me that all that was needed was for someone to live in it and furnish it with the everyday, pleasant thoughts of friendship and cheerfulness and hospitality.

> We all know there is a spirit in every home, a sort of composite spirit . . . formed of the features of different individuals.

We all know there is a spirit in every home, a sort of composite spirit composed of the thoughts and feelings of the members of the family as a composite photograph is formed of the features of different individuals. This spirit meets us at the door as we enter the home. Sometimes it is a friendly, hospitable spirit, and sometimes it is cold and forbidding.

If the members of a home are ill-tempered and quarrelsome, how quickly you feel it when you enter the house. You may not know just what is wrong, but you wish to make your visit short. If they are kindly, generous, good-tempered people, you will have a feeling of warmth and welcome that will make you wish to stay. Sometimes you feel that you must be very prim and dignified, and at another place you feel a rollicking good humor and a readiness to laugh and be merry. Poverty or riches, old-style housekeeping or modern conveniences do not affect your feelings. It is the characters and personalities of the persons who live there.

Each individual has a share in making this atmosphere of the home what it is, but the mother can mold it more to her wishes.

I read a piece of poetry several years ago that was supposed to be a man speaking of his wife, and this was the refrain of the little story:

"I love my wife because she laughs,

Because she laughs and doesn't care."

I'm sure that would have been a delightful home to visit, for a good laugh overcomes more difficulties and dissipates more dark clouds than any other one thing. And this woman was the embodied spirit of cheerfulness and good temper.

Let's be cheerful! We have no more right to steal the brightness out of the day for our own family than we have to steal the purse of a stranger. Let us be as careful that our homes are furnished with pleasant and happy thoughts as we are that the rugs are the right color and texture and the furniture comfortable and beautiful!

Going After the Cows
APRIL 1923

With the birds singing, the trees budding, and "the green grass growing all around," as we used to sing in school, who would not love the country and prefer farm life to any other? We are glad that so much time can be spent out-of-doors while going about the regular affairs of the day, thus combining pleasure with work and adding good health for full measure.

> I have never lost my childhood delight in going after the cows.

I have a favorite way of doing this, for I have never lost my childhood's delight in going after the cows. I still slip away from other things for the sake of the walk through the pastures, down along the creek, and over the hill to the farthest corner where the cows are usually found, as you can all bear witness.

Bringing home the cows is the childhood memory that oftenest recurs to me. I think it is because the mind of a child is peculiarly attuned to the beauties of nature, and the voices of the wildwood, and the impression they made was deep.

"To him who, in the love of nature, holds community with her visible forms, she speaks a various language," you know. And I am sure old Mother Nature talked to me in all the languages she knew when, as a child, I loitered along the cow paths, forgetful of milking time and stern parents waiting, while I gathered wildflowers, waded in the creek, watched the squirrels hastening to their homes in treetops, and listened to the sleepy twitterings of birds.

Wild strawberries grew in grassy nooks in springtime. The wild plum thickets along the creek yielded their fruit about the time of the first frost in the fall. And all the time between, there were ever varied, never failing delights along the cow paths of the old pasture. Many a time, instead of me finding the cows, they, on their journey home unurged, found me and took me home with them.

The voices of nature do not speak so plainly to us as we grow older, but I think it is because, in our busy lives, we neglect her until we grow out of sympathy. Our ears and eyes grow dull, and beauties are lost to us that we should still enjoy.

Life was not intended to be simply a round of work, no matter how interesting and important that work may be. A moment's pause to watch the glory of a sunrise or a sunset is soul satisfying, while a bird's song will set the steps to music all day long.

Home
AUGUST 1923

Out in the meadow, I picked a wild sunflower, and as I looked into its golden heart, such a wave of homesickness came over me that I almost wept. I wanted Mother, with her gentle voice and quiet firmness; I longed to hear Father's jolly songs and to see his twinkling blue eyes; I was lonesome for the sister with whom I used to play in the meadow picking daisies and wild sunflowers.

> The real things of life that are the common possession of us all are of the greatest value.

Across the years, the old home and its love called to me, and memories of sweet words of counsel came flooding back. I realize that all my life the teachings of those early days have influenced me, and the example set by Father and Mother has been something I have tried to follow, with failures here and there, with rebellion at times; but always coming back to it as the compass needle to the star.

So much depends upon the homemakers. I sometimes

wonder if they are so busy now with other things that they are forgetting the importance of this special work. Especially did I wonder when reading recently that there were a great many child suicides in the United States during the last year. Not long ago we never had heard of such a thing in our own country, and I am sure that there must be something wrong with the home of a child who commits suicide.

Because of their importance, we must not neglect our homes in the rapid changes of the present day. For when tests of character come in later years, strength to the good will not come from the modern improvements or amusements few may have enjoyed but from the quiet moments and the "still small voices" of the old home.

Nothing ever can take the place of this early home influence, and as it does not depend upon externals; it may be the possession of the poor as well as of the rich, a heritage from all fathers and mothers to their children.

The real things of life that are the common possession of us all are of the greatest value—worth far more than motor cars or radios, more than lands or money—and our whole store of these wonderful riches may be revealed to us by such a common, beautiful thing as a wild sunflower.

ABOUT THE AUTHOR

Laura Ingalls Wilder (1867–1957) began writing, at age sixty-five, a series of eight children's books about her life in the pioneer West. These books were later turned into a world-renowned TV series. We all came to know and love Laura and her family either through the TV series or through the books. Yet twenty years before she even started the series, Wilder wrote articles for regional newspapers and magazines. *Writings to Young Women* is a collection of these articles.

ABOUT THE EDITOR

Stephen W. Hines has loved Laura Ingalls Wilder's books since he was a boy, and this love is evident in the careful research and arrangement of these delightful articles. Hines graduated from the University of Kansas and received his MA in journalism from Ball State University in Muncie, Indiana. He has worked in publishing since 1979. More than six hundred thousand of his books are currently in print.